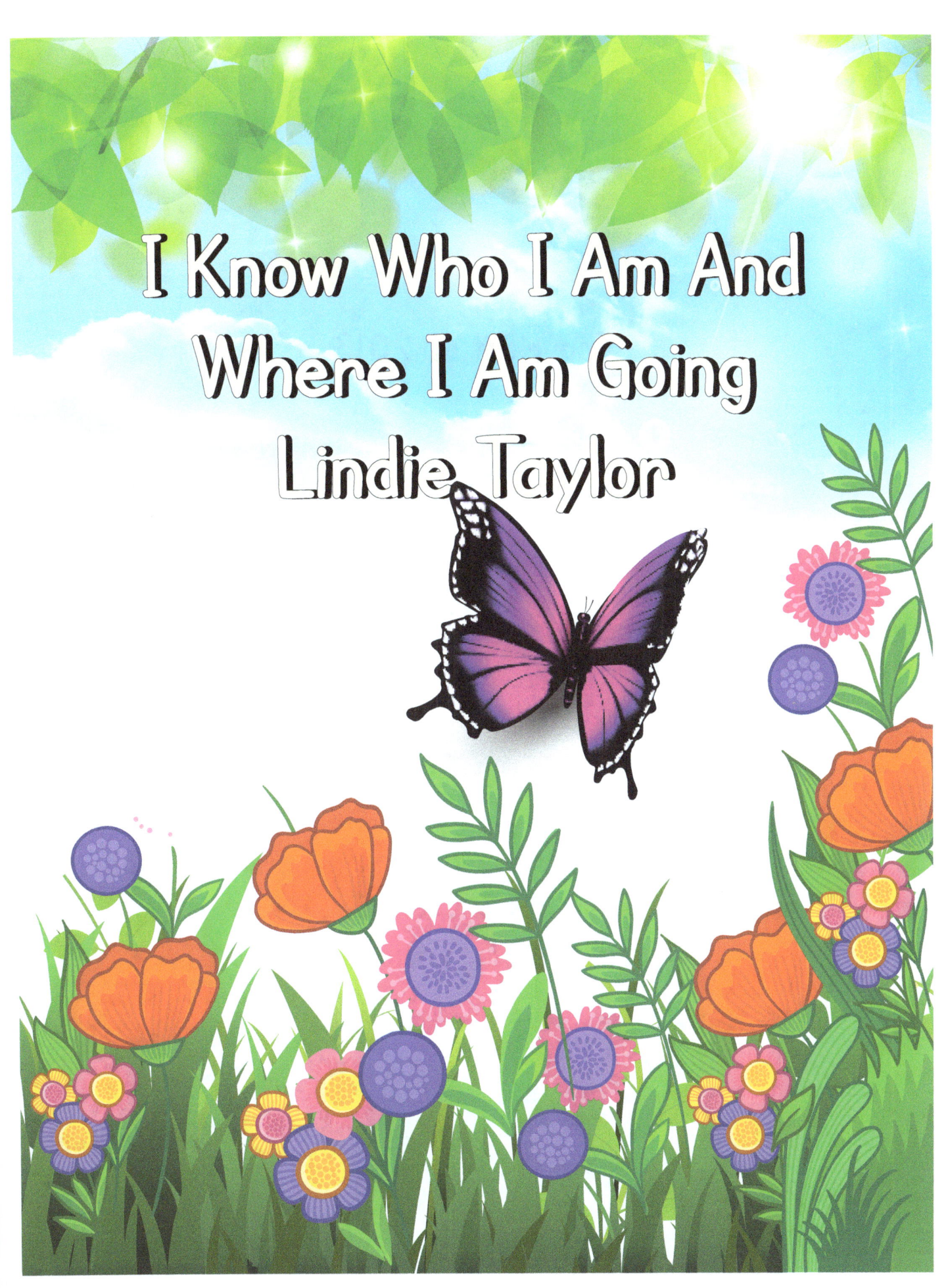

Copyright © 2013

The right of Lindie Taylor to be identified as the author of the work has been asserted by her in accordance with the Copyright Act No. 98 (1987).

ALL RIGHTS RESERVED.

No part of this publication may be reproduced or transmitted in any form by any means, electronic or mechanical, including photocopying and recording, or by any information storage and retrieval system, except as may be expressly permitted in writing from the author.

CONTENTS

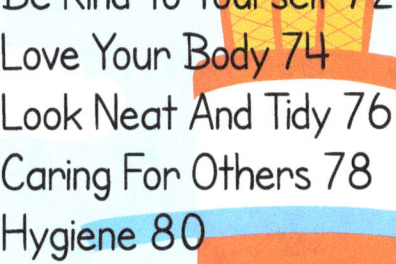

You Are Here For A Reason 10
Your Path 14
Where Do You Fit
Into This World? 16
Your Body 18
Your Brain 24
Your Emotional Side 26
Your Spiritual Side 28
Values 32
Having A Plan 34
Decisions 36
Friends 38
Your Gift 40
Education 42
Reading Power 44
Money 46
Marriage 48
What Is Love? 52
Look After Your Heart 64
Boundaries
Respect 70

Be Kind To Yourself 72
Love Your Body 74
Look Neat And Tidy 76
Caring For Others 78
Hygiene 80
Accepting Others 82
Abuse 86
Verbal Abuse 88
Challenging Times 90
Surrendering Prayer 94
Forgiveness 94
Bullies 96
Rejection And
Gossiping 98
Stress 100
Negative Thoughts 102
Our Planet 104
Plant A Tree 106
A Poem For You 108

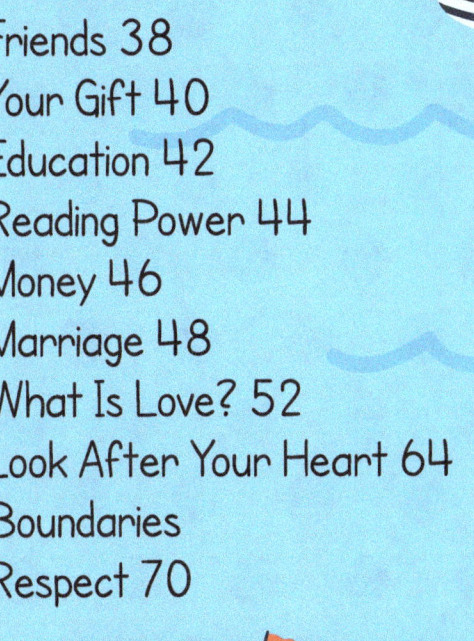

FOREWORD

Lindie's first book, teaching children how to understand their body better, is a total revelation and works hand in hand with this book, giving young people an awareness of who they are and understanding their environment. The world can appear cruel, and young people do not always know how to deal with the challenges life brings. This book is a guide to help young people to understand who they are and what their purpose is in life.

Too many times we assume children are able to deal with emotions they are being confronted with. Most times we do not provide them with the adequate knowledge and tools to understand the basic foundation of how life works, with adverse effects later on in life. I think caring adults should read this book to children and then let them read it for themselves.

A beautifully written book and so clearly needed for young people right now! I cannot recommend this book enough. This book has the ability to empower young children in so many ways. Parents can also benefit by reading this to their children. This book also opens up discussions young children are generally afraid of talking about.

Well done, Lindie! What a fabulous book!

Barkie Mckrea - Author of the book "Do You Need A Life Coach? Social Science Crime Degree Psychology (Honours), Current Masters Citation (Life Coaching)

ACKNOWLEDGEMENTS

A tribute to my Heavenly Father for giving me the vision to write this book.

I am also thankful to my Heavenly Father for allowing my path to cross with Cynthia Tolbert, JD, Of Counsel, Master Life Coach and Natural Health Medic.
email: cynthiatolb@aol.com
Cynthia, your contribution to this journey is invaluable and much appreciated.

A tribute to my Canadian family:
Twyla Grieve,
Wayne Parry, Simona and Alfred Abel,
Rob and Kerry Robertson.
Thank you for believing in this vision and changing my life.

A big thank you to my inspiration, my son Micki Venter.

My Aunt Dawn Hollander, thank you so much for your kindness and wisdom on this journey.

A special dedication to my mom Lorna and my dad Grobbie.

INTRODUCTION

I grew up in an environment that was fairly disruptive. As I grew older and learned about life, I saw the next generation struggling with similar issues that I had growing up.

I decided to write a book to help guide and bring awareness to children about who they are and how living life impacts them.

This book aims at preparing children mentally and emotionally for where they are now and where they are heading in the future.

YOU ARE HERE FOR A REASON

Out of 250 million sperm cells, you won the race!

You are the result of that sperm's race to reach your mom's egg first.

That thought is amazing and something to think about.

Your whole existence is a miracle!

From winning the race out of millions of sperm cells, you started developing from a tiny little cell to a person with a head, body, arms and legs.

This process of developing into a human being is mind boggling.

You are the most amazing design on this planet! Your body is more beautifully designed than any fancy sports car or computer program.

You are unique and special. There is not another you out there. No one has the same fingerprint as you. Your body, your personality and your face is unique to you. Even twins do not have the same fingerprint.

There will never be another you, ever.

 6 Weeks

8 Months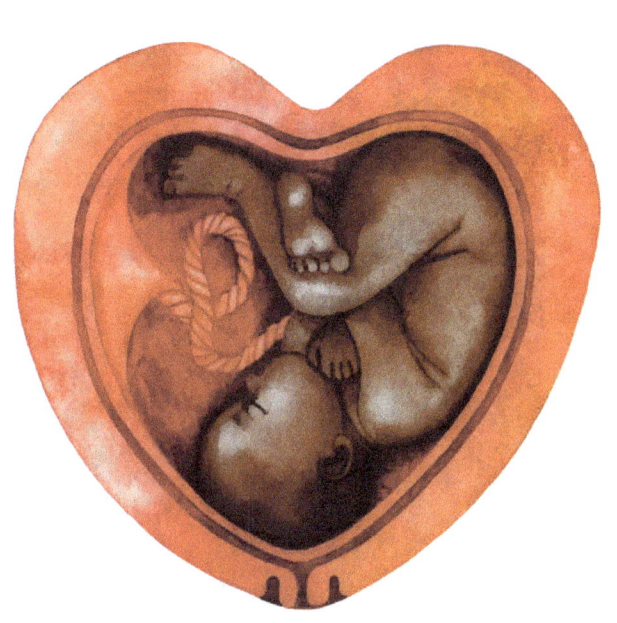

 10 Months

YOUR PATH

Many children, as they grow older, do not know who they are and what their purpose is on Planet Earth. When this happens, you may find as you get older that you are in a job that you do not like. You may choose a husband or a wife that is not compatible. You may find that you feel insecure and confused a lot.

Knowing who you are and where you want to go is extremely important on your journey in life. The sooner you can find out why you are here on Planet Earth, you will find strength, happiness and purpose.

Knowing who you are and where you are going will prevent a lot of wrong turns in your life.

The following pages are designed to assist you in guiding you to discover your purpose.

There will also be tips on what to expect from your journey as you get older.

WHERE DO YOU FIT INTO THIS WORLD?

In most families there is a mom and a dad that look after you. Sometimes you, or even some of your friends, only have a mom or just a dad to look after you.

In some cases your grandma or grandpa is looking after you.

Some children do not even have a mom or a dad or a family.

Having no parents or only one parent to look after you is not easy. However, never forget -- no matter where you are -- you are here for a reason and there is a purpose for you being on Planet Earth.

You need to find out who you are and why you are here.

Let us start discovering who you are.

You consist of FOUR parts:

PHYSICAL
MENTAL
EMOTIONAL
SPIRITUAL

YOUR BODY

Your body is like a machine. Any machine, like a car, needs looking after. If your dad does not clean and look after his car, the car will start having problems.

If you look after a car, it will last a very long time.

A car needs fuel, water and oil to work properly.

If you gave a car soda pop and sugar, it will not drive properly.

Your body is the same.

If you give your body water, healthy food, exercise and good sleep, your body will work well.

Your body will have lots of energy and you will be able to concentrate better.

If you eat sweets, chocolates, soda pops and stay up late, your body will not work properly. You will not have good energy and you may feel depressed a lot.

RESEARCH HAS SHOWN THAT THE FOLLOWING FOODS DO NOT CONTAIN QUALITY (HEALTHY) ENERGY:

Soda pop

White bread

Chips

Sweets & Cookies

Fast food

YOUR BODY NEEDS THE FOLLOWING TO FUNCTION OPTIMALLY:

Water

Exercise

Fruit & Vegetables

Whole Grain Bread

Nuts & Raisins

When you give your body the right food, your body will respond by giving you healthy, lasting energy throughout the day.

Eating correctly keeps your body clean and functioning properly.

Fruit & Veggies

Exercise

Water

MENTAL HEALTH

The second part of who you are is your BRAIN. Your brain is linked to your body. The brain acts like a computer. In order for the brain's computer to work well every day, the brain relies on healthy food and water to work at its best.

One of the most important functions of the brain is to help you make decisions every day.

Your body needs to convert the food you eat into energy and medicine to help the brain function at its best.

If you feed your body junk food that contains little or no medicine, your brain will struggle to function properly. For example: nuts, fruits, vegetables and seeds have specific ingredients that help the brain to work well. If you do not feed your brain the correct food and water, over time you may feel tired, sad or struggle to concentrate.

When you feed your body healthy food and water, your brain will function well.

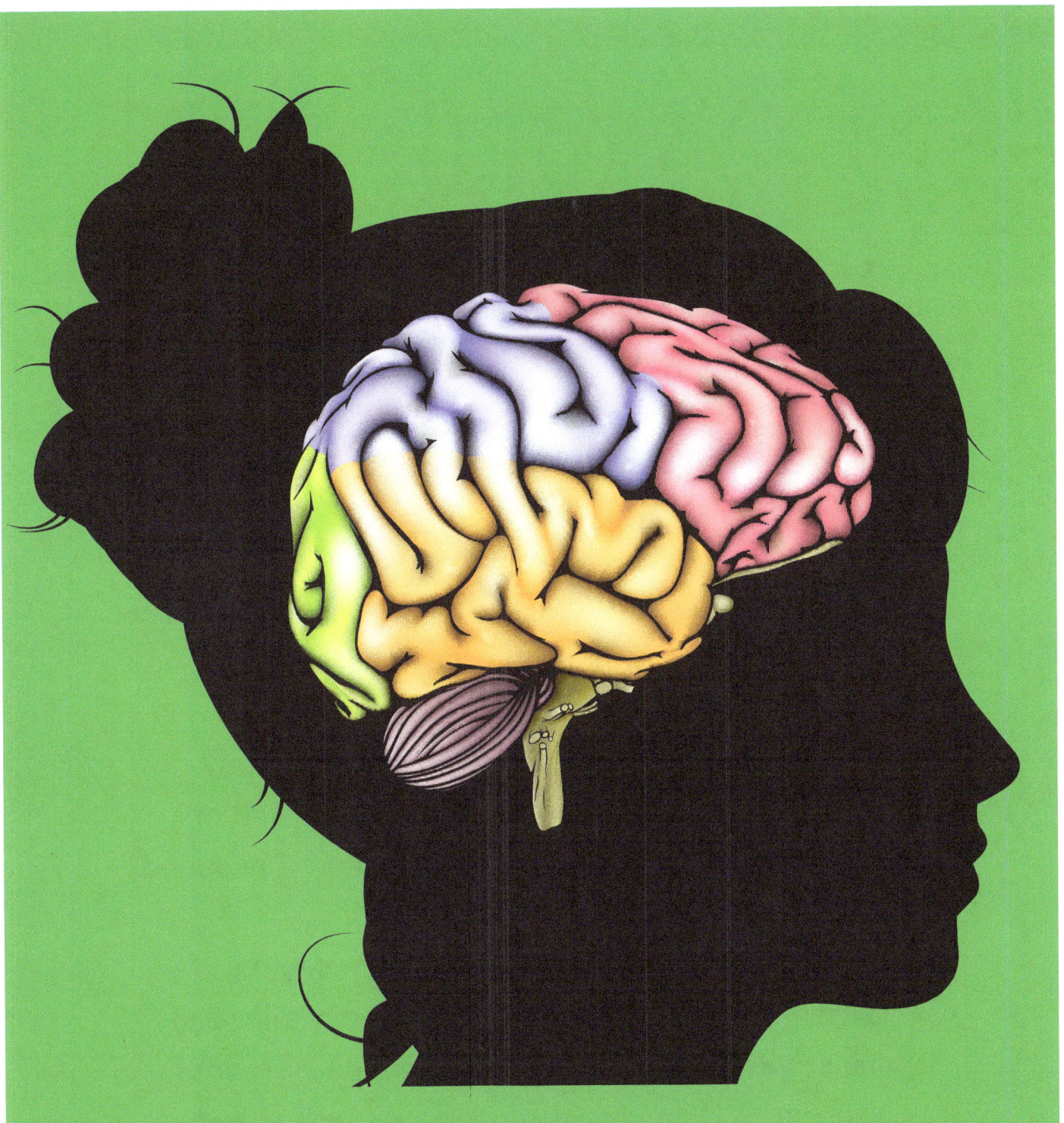

If you want to feel great, drink 8 glasses of water a day. Your brain loves water. Water keeps your brain awake and focused.

YOUR EMOTIONAL SIDE

Your emotional side is the part that makes you feel sad, happy, nervous, or stressed.

Your emotional side is linked to your body and brain. When you feel stressed, sad or afraid, your body and brain are going to respond.

Your body will show sadness by crying. When you are stressed, your brain will send messages to your body that you do not want to eat. If you are scared, you will shiver.

Therefore, if you are emotionally upset, your body and brain will also be upset.

I am feeling great! I am going to the mall this afternoon with my friends.

I did not finish my homework today. Now I am not allowed to go to the mall with my friends.

I ate a lot of sweets at the mall. Now I feel sick!

YOUR SPIRITUAL SIDE

It is important to connect with God. This is your spiritual side. It is important to connect with Him during the good times and the bad times in your life. This gives you balance and builds your character. Staying connected with God is like a little light that constantly shines during the good and the bad times in your life. That little light will never go off. He will constantly guide you to goodness and protect you throughout your life. Many people, as they grow up, feel they have an empty space inside. This empty space can be described as a feeling of loneliness, sadness, and confusion.
Some people choose to fill that empty space with drugs, smoking, and alcohol to make them feel better. However, in the end, those things only make you feel worse.

Most of the time God is the only one that can fill that empty space. All of us have those moments. Here are a few tips you can do to spend time with God and yourself, especially during those lost and confusing times.

I will never leave you nor forsake you.

Ways to spend time with God and yourself.

Take your problems to God. This is a very important part of your spiritual side. You are designed to spend time with God.

Music is very powerful. Research has shown that if you listen to calming music, it can help you feel better.

Walking in nature is very powerful. Nature has the ability to make you feel calm and at peace.

Helping others is a wonderful way to help yourself and others feel better. Helping others is, in a big or in a small way, part of everybody's destiny path.

So far you have learned that you have four parts:

All of these components are connected, and they cannot work on their own.

In the next few pages, we are going to talk about things that happen outside of who you are, that shape who you are inside and out.

VALUES

Since the day you were born your mom and dad taught you what is wrong and what is right.

For example:

> Do not steal.
> Do not gossip.
> Help others.
> Do not lie.

These do's and don'ts your mom and dad taught you are known as good values. Following these good values gives you peace and happiness.

Bad values are as follows:

> I steal.
> I put others down.
> I do not help others.
> I am not helpful.

Following these bad values make you feel unhappy and lonely.

GOOD VALUES

I do not lie.
I do not steal.
I tell the truth.
I am a loyal friend.
I do not gossip.

Having good values helps me to make better decisions. I feel happy when I follow good values.

BAD VALUES

I lie.
I steal.
I am selfish.
I am not a loyal friend.
I gossip.

I did not follow the good values I was taught. Now I feel sad and lost.

HAVE A PLAN

It is very important to have a plan for your life. You need to see where you want to be when you are older.

For example:

Would you like to own a home one day?

What kind of career would you like to have one day?

Do you have an idea of what type of person you would like to marry one day?

Would you like to have children one day?

Do you want to invent something that will help mankind and this planet?

Would you like to make people laugh one day?

Would you like to write a story that inspires people and make a movie out of the story you have written?

When you have an idea of where you want to go in life, you can start working towards it.

There is a saying; "If your dreams do not make you scared, they are not big enough." Write your dreams and plans down in your diary or put them somewhere that you can see them every day.

DREAM AND THINK ABOUT THEM EVERY DAY.

DECISIONS

Decisions are so important. They can actually determine if you will have a happy or an unhappy life.

There are a few important decisions you have to make in your journey called life.

As you get older, you need to make careful decisions regarding the following subjects:

FRIENDS
MARRIAGE
MONEY
RELATIONSHIP WITH YOURSELF
RELATIONSHIPS WITH OTHERS

 Friendship

 Marriage

 Money

 Loving yourself

 Career

 Old Age

FRIENDS

Friends play a very important part in your life.

Friends can convince you that who you are is not good enough and that your good values are boring.

Many people follow their friends and leave their good values behind. In the end, friends could send your life in the wrong direction.

Choose friends that accept you and your values. Do not try and fit into a group of friends that make you turn against your good values.

Choose friends that have the same values, who believe in you and accept you for who you are.

WHAT IS YOUR GIFT? YOUR PASSION?

This is a very important subject. Understanding what is your gifts and passions are is quite simple. You need to ask yourself the question; "What makes me happy, and what do I enjoy doing?" For example: Do you find looking after children makes you feel at peace and content? When you wake up in the morning, you cannot wait to help take care of children. This could be part of your gift, is to look after children to help and guide them.

Do you like numbers and calculations? Do you feel you could happily do math all day and never get tired?

Do you like making people laugh so much that they start crying?

Everyone of us has a gift. When you wish to be like someone else or envy their gift, that only brings sadness into your life. You have your own gift that is unique. Some people have the gift of cooking. Some people have the gift of gardening. Some people have a gift to help other people. Everybody has a gift. You just need to find out what your gift is.

A gift is something you feel happy doing all day long. Sometimes it takes time to find out what your gift is, but once you find it, you will know. Try and make a career from your gift.

When you make your passion your work, it won't feel like work because you enjoy what you're doing.

EDUCATION

Education is very powerful. Look at what you would like to study one day that will enhance your gift, your plans, and your dreams.

Learning helps you understand who you are and what you would like to do with your life one day. Nothing you learn ever goes to waste.

No one can take your knowledge away from you.

The more knowledge you acquire in what you like doing, the clearer your path will shine. For example, if you love working with animals, you learn everything about animals and learn how to help them, and then you will find happiness in your work one day.

READING = POWER

Reading is a powerful way to learn about yourself, your home, planet earth and those around you.

Many times when you do not have the answers to a problem, you may find it in a book.

When nobody understands you, a book can hold answers to questions you may be asking.

Books have the ability to help you with a situation nobody can help you with.

A good habit to have is reading. Reading relaxes you and helps strengthen your brain.

Reading keeps your brain active and prevents your brain from getting lazy.

Books hold many treasures.

The internet is a very powerful tool, but books are just as awesome.

Try going to the library and browsing through the books and reading.

MONEY

There is a saying
"Spend some, save some and give some."
This saying refers to money.

It is important to save money for later in life when you need to stop working.
Many people think they are still young and will save money later in their life for when they are older. Most people fall into this trap and do not save money properly for their old age. Be wise and keep some of your hard-earned money so that when you get older you can relax and enjoy life without having to work and worry about paying bills.

"Spend some" is the nice part about money. However, do not fall into the trap of buying everything on credit. That means you buy something now and sign a contract that you will pay some money every month.

This kind of payment could get you into a lot of trouble, especially if you buy more than you should. You may one day find yourself in a situation where you cannot pay the credit back.
This causes a lot of stress and you could get a bad credit record.
Try your best to save for things you want and pay for the item with cash so that you do not owe anyone a debt.

"Give some" is important. It is important to give some of your earnings to God. This is known as tithing. This is an important habit to have. God will bless your thankful heart bountifully.

MARRIAGE

A time will come when you need to decide if you would like to get married one day. Choosing someone to marry will probably be one of the most important decisions you will ever make.

If you decide to marry the wrong person, it could cause a lot of pain and tears.

Marriage is not easy. Marriage is hard work. You need to be aware of the other person's needs and be able to deal with life's ups and downs.

Marriage is not what the fairy tales tell you. Most girls are taught that a knight in shining armor is going to scoop her up and take her to paradise and live happily ever after.

In most cases this is not true. Love in the real world is also very beautiful but very different from what fairy tales tell you.

Marriage is about accepting the other
person for who they are.

If you choose someone who smokes and drinks when you do not smoke and drink, this may cause problems - especially if you are into health and he is not. Do not think someone will change because they love you. In some cases people do, but in most cases, people are who they are.

They say people who are different from each
other are attracted to each other;
however, people who like the same things
get along better.

Finding someone who has the same values
and interests as you is always a very
good place to start.

WHAT IS LOVE?

Sometimes we are confused about what love is.
We think love is what we see on TV or in movies.
In real life, however, love is quite different.

Faithfulness, kindness, patience, gentleness and being a good listener is part of what love really is.

Love is about loving someone you can talk to about life.
Love is about respecting the other person's personality and funny ways.

Love is loving someone through the good times and the bad times.

Love is not about changing the other person.

Love is not about hurting someone physically or emotionally.

It is important to make a list of the kind of person you would like to marry one day.

Be realistic about the points you put on your list.

Never compromise on these points. If the person you like does not fit your requirements, do not think they will change for you later.

You have to understand that what you see in front of you is not necessarily going to change or get better.

It is important that the person you choose, one day, sees your heart and respects the person you are.

Looking attractive is important. However, good looks change and people grow old.

You want someone that is going to respect and love you no matter what. It is important to spend time with someone. The reason being is that you should have a good idea how that person treats you during good and bad times.

Love takes time. Many people rush into marriage
not knowing the other person well.

If you want true happiness, you
have to wait and get to know the person well.
You must see if he/she has good values or bad values.

Does he/she look after their body?

Does he/she treat their mother and father well?

Would he/she be responsible by keeping a job
to build a future together?

If you're going to marry someone because they are
good looking and say they love you, but they
treat you badly,
you may end up very unhappy.

Marriage is about good communication.

You must feel that you can talk to your husband or wife about the good and the bad situations in life and know that you will be supported.

Communication is very important. If you feel you cannot talk to your boyfriend or girlfriend and they do not really listen to you, it is a warning signal that you need to take note of. Remember that how you are treated during dating will be how you are treated when you are married.

Make sure you can communicate with your boyfriend/girlfriend well, without being scared.

The person you choose for life
should be willing and
wanting to spend quality time with you.

It is important to spend time with each other.

Quality time is key to having a good
marriage one day.

Without quality time, a marriage will start
to have problems because you are pulling away
from each other.

Be on the lookout if your future partner
is willing to make time for you
when life is hectic and busy
or take note if they just squeeze you in.

Marriage is more than just
wearing a ring on your finger.

Marriage is a relationship
that grows over time and makes you a
better person.

Relationships are a way of getting to know
yourself and the other person better.

Marriage should help you grow into a better
person. If not, then there is something
missing.

To have a successful marriage,
you need to be married to yourself first.
You need to love and accept yourself first.
If you do not love and accept yourself, you
could end up hurting
yourself and the other person.

Learn to respect yourself and only expect the
best for yourself and, in turn, you will
attract the same kind of person.

Our intimate relationships should change us
for the better.

LOOK AFTER YOUR HEART

MAKE A DECISION TO CHOOSE GOOD HEALTHY RELATIONSHIPS.

WHENEVER SOMEONE TREATS YOU BADLY, YOU NEED TO BE STRONG ENOUGH TO WALK AWAY AND WAIT FOR THE RIGHT PERSON WHO WILL LOVE AND RESPECT YOU.

After you get married, you may decide to have children.

Children are a precious gift. You need to make sure that you are prepared to look after your precious gift.

Make sure you have a home and food available to look after your child or children.

You will then be a mother or a father. This is possibly the biggest responsibility you will ever have.

Sticking to this responsibility gives your children and your wife/husband the biggest gift ever. You will give your family stability and confidence to face the world.

Breaking this responsibility can cause a lot of problems for you and your family.

BOUNDARIES

The most important thing you can do for yourself is to love and accept yourself.
The second most important thing you can do for yourself is to set boundaries around you so that people will not take advantage of you. For example: Your friend will keep asking you to do her homework if you do not draw a line and say no. Your friend needs to take responsibility for themselves. You are teaching your friend not to value and respect you. Your friend will keep on using you and in the end, you feel very unhappy. Be willing to say no when you feel you have done enough. People will respect you if you say no. People will not respect you if you say yes all the time because they know they can take advantage of you.
In turn, you also need to respect other people's boundaries.

RESPECT

What is respect?
Respect is when you value yourself
and others.

The following pages contain tips how to
respect yourself.

Clean room

Always keep your room clean and be proud
of your little space. This is your space where you
can relax and just be you.

Looking after gifts, clothes, your bike and toys
shows that you respect the things you have because
they belong to you.

When you look after your things, you are giving
yourself positive messages that you are trustworthy
and you will grow older creating trust within yourself
and to those around you.

BE KIND TO YOURSELF

Another way to love and respect yourself
is to give your body a hug now and again.
Your body does so much for you every day.
Your body helps you run and play
with your friends.
Your body helps you clean your room.
There are countless ways how your body
helps you every day.
Your body is very clever and listens to everything
you say. By hugging and giving your
body messages of thanks is a wonderful way
to show respect to yourself.

Most people have problems with their bodies. The magazines and television gives us high expectations that are often not reality. The girls and guys in magazines have their figures photo-shopped so they look thinner or stronger. In real life, most of them do not look like the pictures you see in magazines.

Do not hate your body because your body does not look like people in magazines. Your aim is to be healthy and accept who you are. If you feel that you need to lose weight, be gentle on your body. Eat healthy meals and exercise. Give your body at least 6 months to lose weight. Crash diets do not work. Adopting a healthy lifestyle always works. Drink loads of water and eat your meals slowly.

LOOKING NEAT AND TIDY

Dressing neatly and keeping your hair tidy tells your body and others that you love and respect yourself.

When people see that you love and respect yourself by looking neat and tidy, they will respect you in return.

It is important to not get boastful about how you love yourself.

Self-respect should be cultivated with humbleness and not pride.

CARING FOR OTHERS

When you help others you help yourself.

When you are very stressed and unhappy,
find an older person or someone that is lonely,
and give them some
flowers or chocolates. You will see
your stress and unhappiness lift.

So caring for others helps not only them
but yourself too.

Caring for others is a wonderful gift to give to someone and yourself.

HYGIENE

Nothing looks better than clean,
well-maintained
fingernails and hair.

Making an effort to look after
your hair and
nails makes you feel good and confident.

Cleaning, cutting your nails and smelling
nice is another way of loving and caring
for yourself.

Looking after your body by cleaning your body, cleaning your teeth, your nails and smelling nice is a way of showing your body and yourself that you respect yourself.

ACCEPTING OTHERS

Everybody is different. Nobody is the same.

When you say something bad about someone because they are different, that is not only nasty but also shows you do not love and accept yourself.

Make a list of things you like and a list of things your best friend likes. No one is ever the same, and that is a beautiful thing.

GUT FEELING AND THE SOFT LITTLE VOICE

A gut feeling is a feeling you feel inside of your body when you are uncomfortable about something. You normally will feel it in the middle of your stomach area.

You normally experience a gut feeling when you need to make a decision you are not sure of.

For example, your friends might say to you, "Hey, Mike, let us steal money out of your mom's purse and go play games at the video store. Your mom will never think it is you, and we can have so much fun. Your mom is at your neighbor's house. Come on, let's do it!"

Immediately, you may hear a soft little voice inside your head say, "No, Mike. Your mom and dad did not teach you to steal." During this time you may experience an uneasy feeling in your gut and you become uncomfortable.

You also have another voice in your head that tries to convince you that you must go and steal your mom's money. This voice may say, "Come on, Mike! Just do it once! It will be fun! Do not be so boring!" That is when you will have to make a choice. Normally if you stick to what is right, your friends will admire you for doing the right thing. If you decide to follow your friends and you get into trouble, you can be sure that they are not going to help you out of trouble.

When you have friends that always get you into trouble, they may not be the best friends for you. This is why it is important to love and respect yourself and say no when your gut feeling and the soft little voice says no. Sticking to your good values and listening to your gut feeling normally saves you from a lot of troubles and tears.

ABUSE

There are different kinds of abuse.

When someone makes you feel badly about yourself for no reason at all, this is a form of emotional abuse. Avoid this kind of person immediately. Abusers most times are very insecure people and need to make others feel horrible about themselves in order for them to feel better about themselves. When someone drains you and tries to control you, this is also a form of abuse.

Physical Abuse

When someone physically hurts or touches you and makes you feel uncomfortable, you need to be brave and scream "no" and run! When someone touches you and makes you feel uncomfortable and tells you to keep it a secret, you must be brave and say "I feel uncomfortable. I am leaving now." Immediately find someone you trust and tell them what happened. There are many numbers on the internet that you can call. Whatever you do, be brave. Do not be scared to say NO! Abusers do not like being told no.
They may become angry and try to intimidate you. They will say you are too sensitive and try to convince you that something is wrong with you. Under no circumstances believe those words. Know who you are and do not let anyone make you think or feel bad about yourself. This is a form of abuse. Abusers will try everything to break you down and confuse you so that they can have control over you. Do not let this happen. Search for someone you can speak to until you are heard. Sometimes you are the only one that can protect yourself. This is one of the bravest things you can do for yourself.

If anyone makes you feel sad or uncomfortable, they are probably not good people to be around. Stick to people who make you feel good about life and yourself.

VERBAL ABUSE

Verbal abuse is sometimes worse than physical abuse. Verbal abuse is when someone continuously breaks you down with their mouth by saying nasty things to you.

You can confront the person by stating that if they do not stop their verbal abuse, you will report them to the police for abuse.

If you need evidence, record the verbal abuse without them knowing, using your cell phone. Take the evidence to the police or welfare center as soon as possible.

You can get a restraining order from the court against the person who is verbally or physically abusing you.
A restraining order is when someone is not allowed to come near you or speak to you.

You as an individual have many rights. Be brave and speak out. You will be surprised how much help is out there.

Do whatever you can to protect yourself. Expose any abuse as soon as possible.

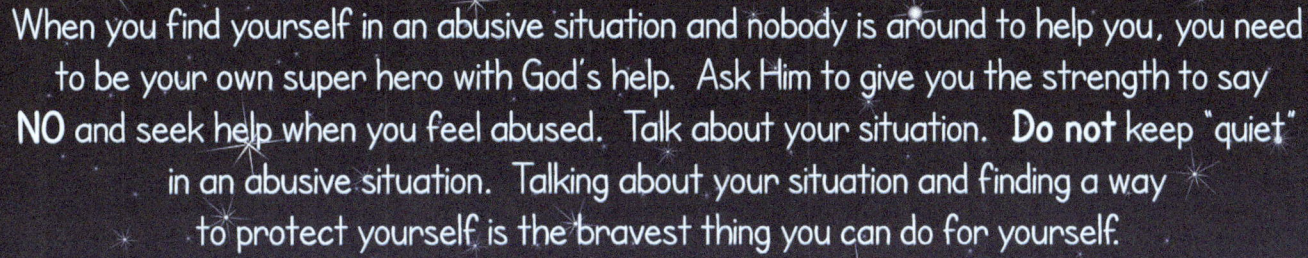

CHALLENGING TIMES

There may come a time in your life when you feel like life is just not worth it anymore.

Most of us at one point in our lives do feel this way. We all have to make a decision when those very difficult times arrive. The question that comes up during those very difficult times is as follows: "Are you going to give up and allow the lying voices in your head to defeat you? Or are you going to stand up and fight the good fight!"

You may ask yourself why should I fight? Here are a few reasons. There are many more. You have been chosen to be here. No matter what your situation is things will change. When you stand up and fight and win for that day you do become stronger. You may not feel it immediately but you do become braver and stronger. This planet needs you. Needs you for what you may ask? This planet needs you for you just to be you. You may help someone by sharing how you stood up and fought for who you are. By sharing your story you help others to stand up and change their lives. There are many other reasons to fight but most importantly you just being you and sharing your battle story is more valuable than you think. This battle is not easy and you cannot do it on your own. You may turn to people, but most of the time people have their own lives and they may drop you when you need them most. Do not take this personally. Life is very distracting and busy.

There is someone, however, that has promised to help you during the tough times and the good times and that is Jesus. The Bible is filled with promises. The Bible says that Jesus even knows the amount of hair on your head. Jesus also said that He will never leave you nor forsake you. All you need to do is to take your problems to Him in prayer and surrender those problems to Him. Big or small give it all to Jesus. The most important thing you have to do is to trust that Jesus will help you. Jesus will help you in His time and not in your time. You may lose hope when He doesn't answer your prayer immediately, but be rest assured Jesus' timing is always perfect. Pray, surrender and trust. Pray surrender and trust. Repeat this every time you start doubting. This process will help you big time.

SURRENDER PRAYER

Dearest Jesus

I come before you feeling lost and confused. I do not know what to do.
You are the only one I have to talk to about this situation. I need your help.

I understand that you do not solve everything my way and in my time.
I understand you solve things in your time.

Jesus, I now surrender this problem to you.
I will trust you to solve this situation for me.

In the, meantime, help me to keep busy with positive things and not to
dwell on the problem even if it means that I have to surrender
this situation to you a few times a day.

I claim all the promises in the Bible that you love
me and that you will never leave me.

Thank you for hearing my prayer.

In Jesus' name I pray.

Amen

FORGIVENESS

Forgiveness is difficult, especially when someone has hurt you so badly that all your hope is gone.

It is important to understand that broken and hurting people hurt other people.

Hurting people want to hurt other people to feel better about their own pain.

In order for you to move forward, the time will come where you will have an opportunity to let go of the past and forgive those who hurt you.

Forgiving the person that hurt you sets you free from the prison of shame and pain.

By not forgiving the other person, you hurt yourself even more and place yourself under that person's world of unforgiveness and pain.

BULLIES

TIPS ON HOW TO DEAL WITH A BULLY

Bullies are people who tease you and make you feel unhappy.

It is very important that you know how to deal with bullies. Bullies will always be there even when you are an adult. When you understand, accept and know who you are, these qualities are the best weapons against a bully.

Bullies are afraid of people that know who they are and are not scared to stand up for themselves. This does take courage. Do not be afraid to ask someone for help.

Do the following simple, yet powerful, exercise.

Draw up a list of who you are.

For example: I am a kind person. I love reading. I have dark hair. I have freckles -- anything you can possibly think of. Write at the bottom of the list "I accept myself exactly the way I am." Place this list where you can see it every day. You may think this is silly, but this technique is very powerful to build self-confidence. Loving, accepting and knowing who you are helps you to live your life with courage and helps you to face your fears.

REJECTION AND GOSSIPING

Everybody experiences rejection. Even the most popular guy or girl at school experiences rejection, just like you. Adults also experience rejection.

There are many reasons why people reject each other. Here are a few examples.

When someone rejects you, they may be jealous of you. You might think and look differently from other people. People feel uncomfortable when someone thinks and looks different. We are not made the same. We are all unique. There is much power in being unique and being true to who you are. When you have said "no" to your friends and stayed true to your gut feeling, some friends may not like that. If they reject you because you said no, then they are not real friends. That is okay. There are many people who will accept you for who you are.

Rejection does hurt, but it does not last. Do not base your whole life on that pain because that person rejected you and transferred their pain over to you. When you do not accept yourself, you can take rejection very badly. You believe and accept the other person's actions and keep the pain inside your heart where it does not belong. Do not let someone else's insecurities and pain ruin your happiness. There are fantastic things awaiting you once you get up and move on. Keep your eyes on your dreams and who you want to be. When you are knocked down, get up and keep going. Never, ever give up. This planet needs you.

Gossiping is also a part of life. Try not to get involved with gossiping at school or in your work place. Gossiping hurts those around you and in the end, you also get hurt. Gossiping brings a lot of drama into your life and can cause a lot of problems you do not want to have.

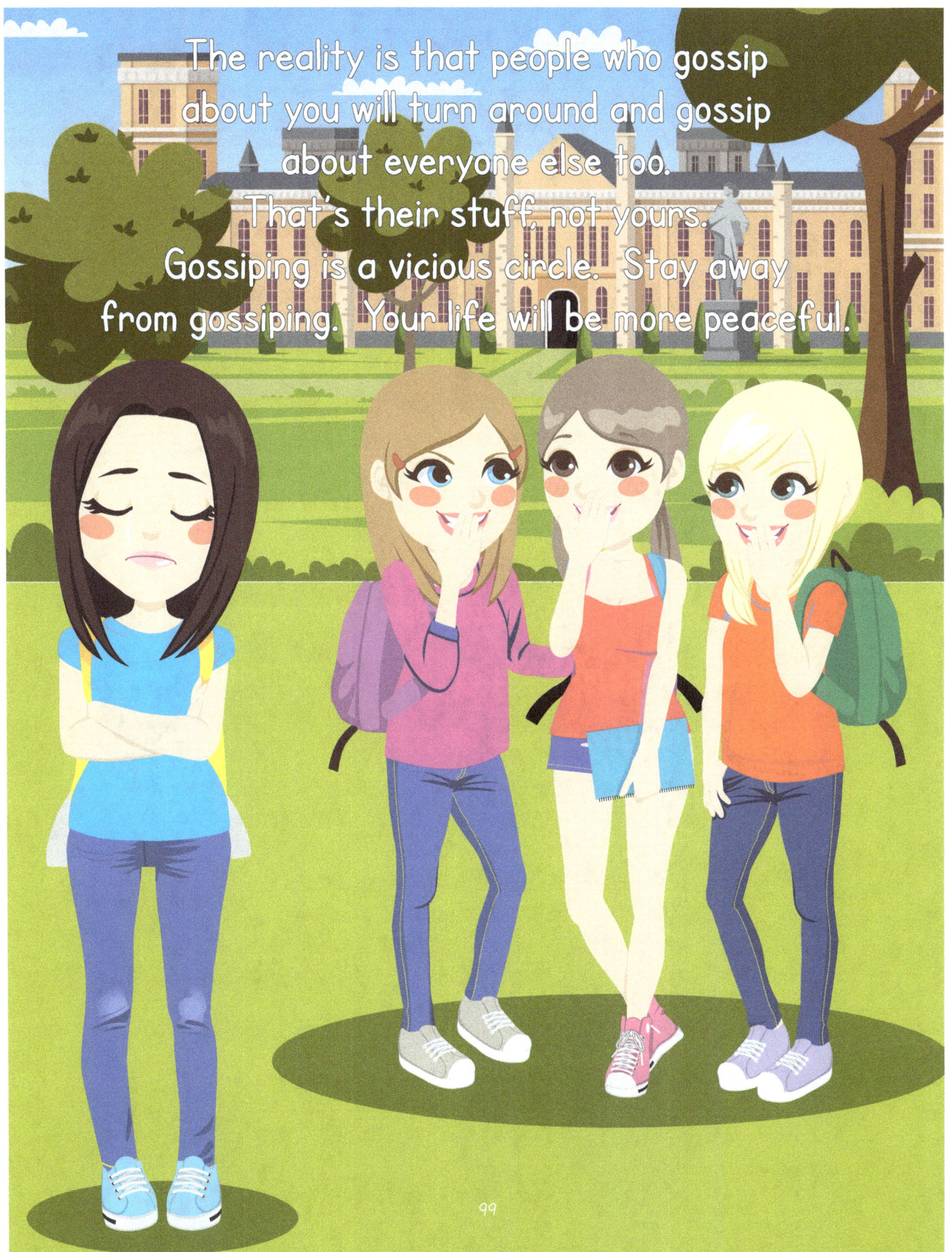

STRESS

Grown-ups and children suffer from stress. Stress is when you are constantly worried.

Stress makes a lot of people sick. Stress can make your life miserable.

Many people, as they grow older, use drugs, food, cigarettes and alcohol to cope with stress.

There are a few ways you can cope with stress naturally.

The following tips are the best ways to deal with stress.

Research has shown that exercise is the best stress reliever. Eat very healthy during stressful times. Your body needs vitamins, especially during stressful times. The vitamins in the healthy foods help your body cope with the stress better.
Drink two litres of water every day.
Take your problems to God and trust Him with your problems. Most things always work out in the end.

Alcohol, drugs, cigarettes and junk food make you forget your worries for a little while but they will destroy you in the end.

Drink lots of water during stressful times. Water has oxygen properties that help your body cope better during stressful times.

Scientists have shown that exercise is one of the most powerful ways to lift depression and stress.

It always feels better chatting to God about problems that nobody is able to help you with.

NEGATIVE THOUGHTS

Be careful of negative thoughts. Most of the time your negative thoughts are not true. If you believe these negative thoughts, they can make you believe things that are not true.

Be in charge of your mind. Think about what you're thinking about. Many times your negative thoughts will talk to you and you need to discipline your mind not to believe these negative words in your head.

It is important to be careful what you watch on TV. TV has the ability to feed your brain information that could affect your mind negatively. The TV tells you that you need to look and act a certain way. The TV is not reality.

You need to form your own identity and do things that will bring you peace and happiness.

OUR PLANET EARTH IS NOT DOING WELL

At the moment our Planet Earth is not doing very well.

Sadly, the biggest reason for this is that people are destroying the Planet Earth at a rapid pace. Your help is desperately needed.

You can make a difference by learning how you can help the planet. If you start helping by doing your little bit, others will follow.

Never, ever underestimate the power of doing the right thing to help this planet. Your help is going to ripple to the farthest corner of Planet Earth without you being aware of it.

You could start a group that creates projects to help Planet Earth. You could create your own super hero club to help save the Planet Earth. You could design your own logo and have a special uniform to create awareness in your neighborhood that you and your friends are actively doing projects to help Planet Earth.

PLANT A TREE

One of the best ways you can help Planet Earth is to plant a tree. A tree is extremely important for the survival of human beings.

Trees are the super heroes of our Planet Earth. They absorb the dirty oxygen and release pure oxygen into the air to help us breathe. Without the oxygen trees produce, we will not be able to survive.

Trees provide us protection against the sun. Planting a tree brings life and happiness.

Trees also supply homes to the birds, spiders, snakes and reptiles and so much more.

Unfortunately, we are cutting down too many trees which supply houses, paper, tables and so much of our daily needs. The trees cannot keep up with our needs and because of this, nature is starting to change in strange ways.

There are so many things you can do to help Planet Earth. Go on the internet to get some ideas. Planet Earth will be so grateful for every little bit of help you and your friends can give.

A POEM FOR YOU

Whenever you look in the mirror,
never underestimate the person that
you see in front of you!

You are unique and an amazing design!

No matter how far anyone travels -- even
into outer space -- there is no one quite
like you!

So embrace all of you,
your spirit, soul and body.

Choose your dreams and never lose
sight of the ever-flickering light....

YOUR DESTINY!

This is a license to life.

<u>BATHABILE DLAMINI</u>
Minister of Social Development (South Africa)

The things my mom always use to say I now read in a book as a guideline to assist my children to start on the right path is fantastic. Kids grow up so much quicker these days and sometimes when mom or dad speak, kids do not always listen, but now I can share this book with my children and help them to accept themselves and embrace their destiny with confidence.

<u>SHANNON LEIGH GROBLER</u>
Medical Insurance Associate, Mother of three boys

This book contains a simple yet powerful message that can be understood by all.

<u>LISA MCINNES</u>
Beauty Specialist, Mother of three boys

Lindie Taylor

President of Awesome Living Corporation
Lifestyle Coach
Colon Irrigation Therapist
International Speaker
Chronic pain Therapist

www.ingramcontent.com/pod-product-compliance
Lightning Source LLC
Chambersburg PA
CBHW081218230426
43666CB00015B/2791